My First Cookbook

For Kids

Delicious Dishes Designed for Junior Cooks

Contents

Introduction 1

Breakfast 3

Lunch 14

Dinner 27

Healthy Snacks 37

Desserts 50

Sides 60

Thank you 69

Introduction

The "My First Cookbook for Kids" website is here. Cooking is a fun adventure full of learning, imagination, and, of course, great food. This guidebook is especially made for aspiring young cooks who are eager to start their culinary journeys.

These pages provide a selection of entertaining, straightforward, and kid-friendly recipes that will not only introduce you to the delights of cooking but also spark a passion for food preparation that will last a lifetime. This cookbook is your ticket to becoming a self-assured and competent cook, whether you're an aspiring chef or a complete newbie in the kitchen.

Cooking is more than just following instructions; it's also about experimenting with flavours and ingredients, as well as serving your dishes to loved ones. The goal of "My First Cookbook for Kids" is to turn cooking into a fun and informative activity where you can use your imagination and gain useful life skills.

You'll find recipes in this cookbook for everything from breakfast to dinner, snacks to desserts, and everything in between. Young cooks may take command in the kitchen with confidence thanks to the meticulous design of each recipe to make it simple to follow.

Breakfast

Banana Split

Ingredients:

1 ripe banana
3 scoops of your favorite ice cream flavors (e.g., chocolate, vanilla, and strawberry)
Chocolate syrup
Strawberry sauce or topping
Crushed pineapple (canned or fresh)
Whipped cream
Chopped nuts (optional)
Maraschino cherries
Sprinkles (optional)

Instructions:

Gather your ingredients: Make sure you have all the necessary ingredients and utensils before starting.

Peel and slice the banana: With the help of an adult, carefully peel the banana and cut it in half lengthwise, creating two long banana halves. Place them in a long dish or on a banana split dish if you have one.

Add the ice cream: Scoop three generous scoops of your favorite ice cream flavors and place them between the banana halves.

Drizzle with sauces: Let the kids drizzle chocolate syrup and strawberry sauce over the ice cream. You can use as much or as little as you like.

Top with pineapple: Add some crushed pineapple over the ice cream and sauces. You can use canned pineapple or fresh pineapple chunks.

Whipped cream: Have the kids add a dollop of whipped cream on top of each scoop of ice cream.

Sprinkle with toppings: If desired, sprinkle some chopped nuts (like walnuts or peanuts) and colorful sprinkles over the whipped cream.

Cherries on top: Finish off your banana split by placing a maraschino cherry on top of each scoop of ice cream.

Serve: Use long spoons and serve your banana split immediately. Enjoy!

Remember to supervise kids when handling sharp objects or hot ingredients, like slicing the banana or drizzling sauces. You can also customize this recipe with different ice cream flavors and toppings to suit your kids' preferences. It's a delicious and creative dessert that's sure to be a hit!

Cinnamon Apple Dippers

Cinnamon Apple Dippers are a simple and tasty snack that kids can easily make with minimal adult supervision. Here's a kid-friendly recipe:

Ingredients:
2-3 apples (any variety)
1 tablespoon lemon juice
(optional, to prevent browning)
1/2 cup granulated sugar
1 teaspoon ground cinnamon
1/4 cup unsalted butter
4-6 whole wheat or white
bread slices
Cooking spray or additional
melted butter for brushing

Instructions:

Ask an adult to help you core and slice the apples into thin wedges or rounds. If you'd like, you can toss them with a tablespoon of lemon juice to prevent browning, although it's not necessary for immediate consumption.

In a small bowl, mix together the granulated sugar and ground cinnamon. Set this mixture aside.

Melt the 1/4 cup of unsalted butter in a microwave-safe bowl or on the stove. Allow it to cool slightly.

Cut the slices of bread into strips or triangles. These will be your dippers.

Brush with Cinnamon Butter:

Lay out the bread slices on a baking sheet or a plate. Use a pastry brush or a spoon to lightly coat one side of each bread piece with the melted cinnamon butter.

Sprinkle the buttered side of the bread with the cinnamon sugar mixture, making sure it sticks to the butter.

Heat a non-stick skillet or griddle over medium heat. Place the bread slices, buttered and sugared side down, onto the hot skillet. Cook for a few minutes on each side until they're golden brown and crispy.

Arrange the toasted cinnamon bread dippers on a plate alongside your sliced apples.

Enjoy: Dip the cinnamon apple slices into the melted cinnamon butter or enjoy them on their own. The toasted cinnamon bread dippers make a delicious complement to the sweet apple slices.

These Cinnamon Apple Dippers are a delightful and wholesome snack that kids can prepare and enjoy. They are perfect for dipping into the buttery cinnamon goodness and pairing with fresh apple slices.

Easy Eggs In A Mug

Ingredients:

2 large eggs
2 tablespoons milk
Salt and pepper, to taste
Optional mix-ins (e.g.,
shredded cheese, diced
vegetables, cooked bacon or
sausage)

Instructions:

Make sure the mug you choose is microwave-safe. It should be large enough to hold two eggs and allow for some expansion without overflowing.

Crack the two eggs into the mug. Be careful not to get any eggshell in the mug.

Pour in the milk, and add a pinch of salt and pepper to taste. Use a fork or small whisk to beat the eggs and milk together until well combined.

If you'd like to add any mix-ins, such as shredded cheese, diced vegetables, or cooked bacon or sausage, now is the time to add them to the mug. Stir everything together to distribute the mix-ins evenly.

Place the mug in the microwave. Cook the eggs on high for 1 minute.

Carefully remove the mug from the microwave (it will be hot). Use a fork to stir the eggs gently. If there are any uncooked parts, return the mug to the microwave and cook in 15-30 second increments, checking and stirring after each interval, until the eggs are fully cooked but still slightly moist. Be cautious not to overcook, as the eggs can become rubbery.

Allow the Eggs in a Mug to cool for a minute or so before serving. Enjoy your easy and quick eggs right from the mug!

This recipe is highly customizable, so kids can get creative with their favorite ingredients. Just make sure they use oven mitts or a towel to handle the hot mug and supervise them while using the microwave to ensure their safety.

Chunky Monkey Oatmeal Balls

Ingredients:

1 ripe banana
1 cup old-fashioned rolled oats
1/4 cup peanut butter (or any nut or seed butter of choice)
1/4 cup chocolate chips (semi-sweet or milk chocolate)
1/4 cup chopped nuts (walnuts, pecans, or your choice)
1 tablespoon honey (optional, for added sweetness)
1/2 teaspoon vanilla extract (optional)

Instructions:
Mash the Banana:
Peel the ripe banana and place it in a mixing bowl. Use a fork to mash it until it's smooth.
Add the old-fashioned rolled oats, peanut butter (or your chosen nut or seed butter), chocolate chips, chopped nuts, honey (if using), and vanilla extract (if using) to the mashed banana. Mix everything together until it's well combined. The mixture should be sticky and easily moldable.
Scoop out small portions of the mixture and roll them between your palms to form bite-sized balls. You can make them as big or as small as you like
Place the oatmeal balls on a plate or tray lined with parchment paper. Once you've formed all the balls, put them in the refrigerator for about 20-30 minutes to firm up.
After chilling, your Chunky Monkey Oatmeal Balls are ready to enjoy. You can eat them right away or store them in an airtight container in the refrigerator for a snack on the go.
These Chunky Monkey Oatmeal Balls are not only tasty but also a healthier alternative to store-bought snacks. Kids can have fun making them and will love the combination of banana, chocolate, and nuts. Feel free to customize the recipe by adding dried fruits, coconut flakes, or other ingredients your kids enjoy.

Pancake in a Mug

Ingredients:

4 tablespoons all-purpose flour
1 tablespoon granulated sugar
1/4 teaspoon baking powder
A pinch of salt
3 tablespoons milk
1/2 tablespoon vegetable oil or
melted butter
1/4 teaspoon vanilla extract
(optional)
Maple syrup, whipped cream, or
your favorite pancake toppings

Instructions:

Select a microwave-safe mug that's large enough to prevent overflowing but not too big, so the pancake rises properly.

In the mug, combine the all-purpose flour, granulated sugar, baking powder, and a pinch of salt. Stir these dry ingredients together with a fork.

Pour in the milk, vegetable oil or melted butter, and vanilla extract (if using). Mix everything well with a fork until the batter is smooth.

Place the mug in the microwave. Cook the pancake on high for 1 minute and 30 seconds to 2 minutes. The exact time may vary depending on your microwave's wattage. Watch it carefully to ensure it doesn't overflow. The pancake should rise and firm up.

Use a fork or toothpick to check the center of the pancake. If it comes out clean, the pancake is ready. If not, you can microwave it for another 10-20 seconds until it's cooked through.

Carefully remove the mug from the microwave (it will be hot), and let it cool for a minute or two. Top your pancake in a mug with maple syrup, whipped cream, or any other favorite pancake toppings.

Use a fork to dig into your pancake in a mug and savor your homemade treat!

This Pancake in a Mug recipe is quick, easy, and perfect for kids who want a tasty breakfast or snack. Just remind them to handle the hot mug with care and always use oven mitts or a towel when removing it from the microwave.

Cinnamon Roll Waffles

Ingredients:
For the Waffle Batter:
1 cup all-purpose flour
1 tablespoon granulated sugar
1 teaspoon baking powder
1/2 teaspoon baking soda
1/4 teaspoon salt
1 cup buttermilk
1 large egg
2 tablespoons unsalted butter, melted
1 teaspoon vanilla extract
For the Cinnamon Roll Swirl:
2 tablespoons unsalted butter, melted
1/4 cup brown sugar
1 teaspoon ground cinnamon
For the Cream Cheese Glaze:
2 tablespoons cream cheese, softened
2 tablespoons powdered sugar
1-2 tablespoons milk
1/2 teaspoon vanilla extract

Instructions:
Preheat your waffle iron according to the manufacturer's instructions.
In a small bowl, combine the melted butter, brown sugar, and ground cinnamon. Mix well to create a cinnamon roll swirl mixture.
In a large mixing bowl, whisk together the flour, granulated sugar, baking powder, baking soda, and salt.
In a separate bowl, whisk together the buttermilk, egg, melted butter, and vanilla extract.
Pour the wet ingredients into the dry ingredients and stir until just combined. Be careful not to overmix; a few lumps are okay.
Pour a portion of the waffle batter into the preheated waffle iron.
Drizzle a spoonful of the cinnamon roll swirl mixture over the batter.
Add another layer of waffle batter on top.
Close the waffle iron and cook according to your waffle iron's instructions until the waffles are golden brown and cooked through.
While the waffles are cooking, prepare the cream cheese glaze. In a small bowl, combine the softened cream cheese, powdered sugar, milk (start with 1 tablespoon), and vanilla extract. Mix until smooth and drizzle-able. If needed, add more milk to achieve your desired consistency.
Once the waffles are ready, transfer them to a plate. Drizzle the cream cheese glaze over the warm waffles.
Serve the Cinnamon Roll Waffles immediately, and enjoy your delicious, homemade treat!
These Cinnamon Roll Waffles are a delightful twist on traditional waffles and are sure to be a hit with kids and adults alike. Just be sure to supervise kids when using the waffle iron to ensure their safety.

Easy Breakfast Pizza

Ingredients:
For the Pizza Crust:
1 pre-made pizza crust (store-bought or homemade)
1/4 cup pizza sauce or tomato sauce
1 cup shredded mozzarella cheese
2-3 large eggs
Salt and pepper to taste
Optional toppings: diced bell peppers, cooked sausage, cooked bacon, diced tomatoes, sliced mushrooms, or any other favorite toppings

Instructions:
Preheat your oven according to the instructions on the pizza crust package, usually around 400°F (200°C).
If you're using store-bought pizza dough, follow the package instructions for prepping and rolling out the dough. If you're using a pre-made pizza crust, you can skip this step.
Place the pizza crust on a baking sheet or pizza stone if you have one.
Spread the pizza sauce evenly over the crust, leaving a small border around the edges for the crust.
Sprinkle the shredded mozzarella cheese over the sauce.
If you want to add toppings, scatter them over the cheese. Kids can get creative and choose their favorite toppings
Carefully crack the eggs onto the pizza, evenly spacing them out. Make small wells or indentations in the cheese and toppings to hold the eggs in place.
Sprinkle a pinch of salt and pepper over the eggs and the toppings.
Place the pizza in the preheated oven and bake for about 12-15 minutes or until the eggs are cooked to your liking. Keep an eye on it to prevent overcooking.
Remove the breakfast pizza from the oven and let it cool for a minute or two.
Use a pizza cutter or a knife to slice the pizza into wedges or squares.
Serve your Easy Breakfast Pizza while it's still warm and enjoy a delicious breakfast!
Kids can have a blast customizing their breakfast pizza with their favorite ingredients. It's a tasty and creative way to start the day. Be sure to supervise them when using the oven and handling hot pans for safety.

Banana Peanut Butter Snack

Ingredients:

1 banana
2 tablespoons peanut butter (or any nut or seed butter of choice)
Toppings of your choice (e.g., chocolate chips, raisins, chopped nuts, honey, or sliced strawberries)

Instructions:
Peel the banana and place it on a plate or cutting board.
Using a kid-safe knife, have your child slice the banana into rounds or lengthwise into halves or quarters, depending on their preference.
Using a butter knife or a child-friendly spreading utensil, let your child spread peanut butter onto the banana slices. They can spread it evenly on one side or create a design if they like.
Encourage your child to add their favorite toppings. Chocolate chips, raisins, chopped nuts, honey, or sliced strawberries are all great options. They can get creative with their choices.
Once the banana slices are topped with peanut butter and their favorite toppings, serve the Banana Peanut Butter Snack immediately.
Your child can now enjoy their delicious and nutritious snack.
This snack is not only tasty but also provides a good balance of healthy fats, carbohydrates, and protein. It's a great way to involve kids in the kitchen and allow them to personalize their snack to their liking. Just ensure they use age-appropriate utensils and supervise them as needed for safety.

Breakfast Cereal Parfait

Ingredients:
1 cup of Greek yogurt (or your choice of yogurt)
1/2 cup of your favorite breakfast cereal
1/2 cup of fresh berries (e.g., strawberries, blueberries, raspberries)
1 tablespoon honey or maple syrup (optional, for added sweetness)
1/4 teaspoon vanilla extract (optional)
Sliced bananas or other fruit (optional)
Chopped nuts or granola (optional)

Instructions:

Prepare the Ingredients:
Wash and chop any fresh berries you plan to use. Set them aside.
If your child prefers sweeter yogurt, they can mix the Greek yogurt with honey or maple syrup in a small bowl. Add the vanilla extract if desired. Stir well to combine.
In a clear glass or a bowl, start by adding a spoonful of the sweetened yogurt or plain yogurt if you're not using sweeteners.
Next, add a layer of cereal on top of the yogurt.
Follow this with a layer of fresh berries.
Repeat the layers until you've used up all your ingredients or reached your desired parfait size.
If your child likes, they can add sliced bananas or any other favorite fruits as additional layers or on top of the parfait.
You can also sprinkle some chopped nuts or granola for added crunch and flavor.
Serve the Breakfast Cereal Parfait immediately.
Grab a spoon and enjoy this healthy and tasty breakfast treat!
This Breakfast Cereal Parfait is a great way to involve kids in making their breakfast and encourages them to choose healthy ingredients. It's also a fun and colorful way to start the day. Make sure to assist younger children when using sharp utensils and handling glassware.

Breakfast Banana Sushi

Ingredients:

1 banana
2-3 tablespoons peanut butter
(or any nut or seed butter of
choice)
2-3 tablespoons granola
2-3 tablespoons diced
strawberries (or any other
favorite fruit)
1-2 tablespoons honey (optional,
for drizzling)
Mini chocolate chips (optional,
for extra sweetness)

Instructions:

Peel the banana and place it on a plate or cutting board.
Using a child-safe knife or a butter knife, have your child spread a layer of peanut butter evenly over the entire banana. Make sure the peanut butter sticks to the banana.
Sprinkle the granola evenly over the peanut butter-covered banana. The granola will stick to the peanut butter.
Let your child place the diced strawberries (or other fruit of their choice) along one side of the banana.
Carefully roll the banana with the toppings up, starting from the side with the fruit. Keep rolling until you have a banana sushi roll.
Use a child-safe knife or a butter knife to slice the banana sushi roll into bite-sized pieces.
Drizzle with Honey (Optional):
If your child wants a little extra sweetness, they can drizzle honey over the banana sushi pieces.
Add Optional Chocolate Chips (Optional):
For a touch of chocolate sweetness, your child can sprinkle mini chocolate chips over the banana sushi
Place the Breakfast Banana Sushi on a plate and serve it immediately.
Your child can now enjoy their delicious and creative breakfast banana sushi!
This Breakfast Banana Sushi is not only tasty but also visually appealing, making it a fun and healthy way to start the day. It allows kids to be creative with their breakfast and choose their favorite toppings. Just be sure to supervise them when using knives and handling utensils for safety.

13

Lunch

Whole-Wheat Veggie Wrap

Ingredients:
For the Veggie Wrap:
1 whole-wheat tortilla or wrap
2-3 tablespoons hummus (or your favorite spread)
1/2 cup mixed vegetables (e.g., bell peppers, cucumber, carrot sticks, lettuce, or any other favorite veggies), thinly sliced or chopped
1/4 cup shredded cheese (optional)
1/4 cup cooked quinoa or brown rice (optional)
Sliced avocado or guacamole (optional)
Sprouts or fresh herbs (optional)
Salt and pepper to taste

Instructions:
Lay out a whole-wheat tortilla or wrap on a clean surface.
Using a spoon, spatula, or butter knife, have your child spread a generous layer of hummus (or another favorite spread like cream cheese or yogurt-based dressing) evenly across the center of the tortilla, leaving a border around the edges.Let your child place the sliced or chopped mixed vegetables on top of the hummus. They can get creative with their veggie choices and arrange them however they like.
If your child enjoys cheese, cooked quinoa or brown rice, avocado slices, or fresh herbs like sprouts, they can add these ingredients on top of the veggies.
Sprinkle a pinch of salt and pepper over the vegetables and optional ingredients for added flavor.
Now, it's time to roll up the wrap. Fold in the sides of the tortilla and then roll it up tightly from the bottom to create a wrap.
Use a sharp knife to cut the Whole-Wheat Veggie Wrap in half diagonally or into smaller bite-sized portions.
Place the wrap on a plate and serve it immediately.
Your child can enjoy their nutritious and delicious Whole-Wheat Veggie Wrap for lunch or as a healthy snack.

Tortilla Pepperoni Pizza

Ingredients:
1 large flour tortilla
2-3 tablespoons pizza sauce
1/2 cup shredded mozzarella cheese
10-12 slices pepperoni
Optional toppings: sliced bell
peppers, sliced olives, sliced
mushrooms, or any other favorite
pizza toppings
Olive oil (for brushing)
Dried oregano or Italian seasoning
(optional)
Red pepper flakes (optional, for
added spice)

Instructions:
Preheat the Oven:
Preheat your oven to 375°F (190°C).
Line a baking sheet with parchment paper to prevent sticking.
Place the flour tortilla on the prepared baking sheet.
Spread a thin layer of pizza sauce evenly over the tortilla, leaving a small border around the edges for the crust.
Sprinkle shredded mozzarella cheese evenly over the sauce.
Add the pepperoni slices and any other desired toppings. Let kids get creative with their choices.
If your child likes, sprinkle a pinch of dried oregano or Italian seasoning over the pizza for extra flavor.
For a bit of spice, you can also add a pinch of red pepper flakes.
Lightly brush the exposed edges of the tortilla with a little olive oil. This will help them crisp up in the oven.
Place the baking sheet in the preheated oven and bake for about 8-10 minutes or until the cheese is melted, and the edges of the tortilla are golden and crisp.
Carefully remove the Tortilla Pepperoni Pizza from the oven using oven mitts. Let it cool for a minute or two.
Use a pizza cutter or a knife to slice the pizza into wedges or squares.
Serve the pizza slices while they're hot and enjoy your homemade Tortilla Pepperoni Pizza!

Toaster-Oven Quesadillas

Ingredients:
2 flour tortillas (6-8 inches in diameter)
1/2 cup shredded cheese (cheddar, mozzarella, or your favorite)
1/4 cup cooked and shredded chicken (optional)
2 tablespoons salsa (optional)
1 tablespoon chopped fresh cilantro (optional)
Cooking spray or a small amount of melted butter

Instructions

If you're using cooked chicken, shred it and have it ready. Also, gather your tortillas, shredded cheese, salsa, and cilantro.

Preheat the toaster oven to 350°F (175°C) and set it to the 'toast' function.

Lay one tortilla flat on a clean surface. Sprinkle half of the shredded cheese evenly over one half of the tortilla.

If using chicken, add the shredded chicken on top of the cheese

Optionally, spoon salsa and sprinkle cilantro over the chicken.

Fold the tortilla in half to cover the ingredients, creating a half-moon shape.

Lightly grease the toaster oven tray or rack with cooking spray or melted butter to prevent sticking.

Place the prepared quesadilla on the toaster oven tray.

Toast the quesadilla in the preheated toaster oven for about 5-7 minutes or until the cheese is melted and the tortilla is crispy and golden brown. Keep an eye on it to prevent burning.

Carefully remove the toaster oven quesadilla (it will be hot) and let it cool for a minute or two.

Use a knife or pizza cutter to slice the quesadilla into wedges or triangles.

Plate the quesadilla slices and serve them immediately.

Kids can now enjoy their homemade Toaster Oven Quesadillas with their favorite dipping sauce, such as salsa or sour cream.

Veggie & Hummus Sandwich

Ingredients:
2 slices of whole-grain bread or your favorite bread
2-3 tablespoons hummus (your choice of flavor)
1/4 cup cucumber slices
1/4 cup bell pepper strips (red, green, or both)
1/4 cup carrot sticks or shredded carrots
1-2 lettuce leaves
1-2 slices of tomato (optional)
Salt and pepper to taste
Sliced avocado or sprouts (optional)
Cheese slices (optional)
Mustard or mayonnaise (optional)

Instructions:

Prepare the Ingredients:
Wash and prepare the vegetables by slicing the cucumber, bell pepper, and carrot sticks. Set them aside.
Lay out the two slices of bread on a clean surface.
Spread a generous layer of hummus on one or both slices of bread, depending on your preference.
Place the lettuce leaves on one slice of bread.
Add the cucumber slices, bell pepper strips, and carrot sticks on top of the lettuce.
If you like, add tomato slices, avocado, sprouts, or cheese slices for extra flavor and texture.
Sprinkle a pinch of salt and pepper over the vegetables for added flavor.
If desired, add a small amount of mustard or mayonnaise to the other slice of bread for extra creaminess.
Carefully bring the two slices of bread together to close the sandwich.
Slice and Serve:
Use a sharp knife to cut the Veggie & Hummus Sandwich in half diagonally or into smaller pieces for easier handling.
Serve the sandwich immediately and enjoy your healthy and tasty meal!

Cream Cheese & Veggie Roll-Up

Ingredients:
1 large flour tortilla or a spinach or tomato-flavored tortilla
2-3 tablespoons cream cheese (plain or flavored)
1/4 cup thinly sliced bell peppers (red, green, or both)
1/4 cup thinly sliced cucumber
1/4 cup thinly sliced carrots
1-2 lettuce leaves
Salt and pepper to taste
Optional: thinly sliced avocado, sprouts, shredded cheese, or any other favorite veggies or toppings

Instructions:
Prepare the Ingredients
Wash and prepare the vegetables by slicing the bell peppers, cucumber, and carrots into thin strips. Set them aside.
Lay out the flour tortilla on a clean surface.
Spread a layer of cream cheese evenly over the entire surface of the tortilla, leaving a small border around the edges.
Layer the Vegetables:
Place the lettuce leaves on top of the cream cheese.
Add the thinly sliced bell peppers, cucumber, and carrots on top of the lettuce. You can also add any other preferred veggies or toppings.
Sprinkle a pinch of salt and pepper over the vegetables for added flavor.
If you like, you can add thinly sliced avocado, sprouts, or shredded cheese.
Carefully roll up the tortilla tightly from the bottom, tucking in the sides as you go to create a compact roll.
Use a sharp knife to cut the Cream Cheese & Veggie Roll-Up into bite-sized pieces or larger sections, depending on your preference.
Enjoy:
Serve the roll-up immediately and enjoy your tasty and healthy snack or meal!

Pizza Roll-Up

Ingredients:
1 large flour tortilla (10 inches in diameter)
2-3 tablespoons pizza sauce
1/2 cup shredded mozzarella cheese
10-12 slices pepperoni (or any preferred pizza toppings)
Optional: sliced bell peppers, sliced olives, sliced mushrooms, or any other favorite pizza toppings
Olive oil (for brushing)
Dried oregano or Italian seasoning (optional)
Red pepper flakes (optional, for added spice)

Instructions:
Preheat the Oven:
Preheat your oven to 375°F (190°C).
Prepare the Tortilla:
Lay out the large flour tortilla on a clean surface.
Spread a thin layer of pizza sauce evenly over the entire surface of the tortilla, leaving a small border around the edges for the crust.
Layer the Cheese and Toppings:
Sprinkle the shredded mozzarella cheese evenly over the sauce.
Add the pepperoni slices and any other desired pizza toppings. Let kids get creative with their choices.
If your child likes, sprinkle a pinch of dried oregao or Italian seasoning over the pizza for extra flavor.
For a bit of spice, you can also add a pinch of red pepper flakes.
Carefully roll up the tortilla tightly from the bottom, tucking in the sides as you go to create a compact roll.
Lightly brush the outside of the pizza roll-up with a little olive oil. This will help it become crispy when baked.
Place the pizza roll-up on a baking sheet or directly on the oven rack.
Bake in the preheated oven for about 10-12 minutes or until the cheese is melted, and the roll-up is crispy and golden brown.
Carefully remove the pizza roll-up from the oven (it will be hot) and let it cool for a minute or two.
Use a sharp knife to slice the Pizza Roll-Up into bite-sized pieces or larger sections, depending on your preference.
Plate the pizza roll-up slices and serve them immediately.
Your kids can now enjoy their homemade Pizza Roll-Ups with their favorite dipping sauce, such as additional pizza sauce or ranch dressing.

Strawberry & Cream Cheese Sandwich

Ingredients:
2 slices of bread (your choice,
but whole wheat or multigrain
works well)
2-3 tablespoons cream cheese
(plain or strawberry-flavored)
4-5 fresh strawberries,
washed, hulled, and thinly
sliced
Honey (optional, for added
sweetness)
A sprinkle of powdered sugar
(optional, for garnish)

Instructions:
Prepare the Ingredients:
Wash the strawberries, remove the stems (hulls), and thinly slice them. Set them aside.
Lay out the two slices of bread on a clean surface.
Spread a layer of cream cheese evenly on one side of each slice of bread.
Arrange the thinly sliced strawberries on top of the cream cheese on one of the bread slices.
Make sure to cover the entire surface with strawberries.
If your child prefers a sweeter sandwich, drizzle a small amount of honey over the
strawberries. This step is optional, as the sweetness of the strawberries and cream cheese
should be sufficient for most kids.
Top with the Other Slice:
Carefully place the other slice of bread with cream cheese on top of the strawberries to create a
sandwich.
If desired, you can sprinkle a small amount of powdered sugar over the top of the sandwich for
a touch of sweetness and a decorative finish:
Use a knife to cut the Strawberry & Cream Cheese Sandwich into halves or quarters, depending
on your preference.
Serve the sandwich immediately and enjoy your delicious, fruity treat!

Chicken pesto wrap

Ingredients:
1 large flour tortilla
1/2 cup cooked chicken breast,
thinly sliced or shredded (you
can use leftover rotisserie
chicken or grilled chicken)
2-3 tablespoons pesto sauce
(store-bought or homemade)
1/4 cup shredded mozzarella
cheese
1/4 cup sliced cherry tomatoes
A handful of fresh spinach
leaves
Salt and pepper to taste

Instructions:
Prepare the Ingredients:
Cook and shred the chicken if it's not already prepared. Wash and slice the cherry tomatoes and set them aside. Wash the spinach leaves and pat them dry.
Lay the flour tortilla on a microwave-safe plate and heat it in the microwave for about 10-15 seconds to make it more pliable for rolling
Lay the warmed tortilla flat on a clean surface.
Spread a layer of pesto sauce evenly over the entire surface of the tortilla, leaving a small border around the edges.
Place the thinly sliced or shredded chicken evenly on top of the pesto sauce.
Sprinkle shredded mozzarella cheese over the chicken.
Add sliced cherry tomatoes and fresh spinach leaves on top of the cheese.
Sprinkle a pinch of salt and pepper over the veggies for added flavor.
Carefully roll up the tortilla tightly from the bottom, tucking in the sides as you go to create a compact wrap.
Use a sharp knife to slice the Chicken Pesto Wrap in half diagonally or into smaller pieces for easier handling.
Serve the wrap immediately, and enjoy your delicious and nutritious Chicken Pesto Wrap!

Bean & Cheese Burritos

Ingredients:

4 large flour tortillas
1 can (15 ounces) of refried beans
1 cup shredded cheddar or Mexican blend cheese
1/2 cup diced tomatoes (optional)
1/4 cup diced onions (optional)
1/4 cup chopped fresh cilantro (optional)
Sour cream or salsa for serving (optional)

Instructions:
Prepare the Ingredients:
If using diced tomatoes, onions, and cilantro, have them prepared and set aside.
To make the tortillas more pliable, you can warm them in the microwave for about 10-15 seconds each or in a dry skillet for a few seconds on each side.
Lay out one tortilla at a time on a clean surface.
Spread a generous portion of refried beans (about 1/4 of the can) evenly over the entire surface of the tortilla, leaving a small border around the edges.
Sprinkle shredded cheese evenly over the beans.
If you like, add diced tomatoes, onions, and cilantro on top of the cheese.
Carefully fold in the sides of the tortilla.
Roll up the tortilla tightly from the bottom, tucking in the sides as you go to create a compact burrito.
You can serve the burrito as is, or if you prefer it warm, you can heat it in the microwave for about 30 seconds to melt the cheese. Alternatively, you can heat it in a skillet over low heat for a few minutes on each side until it's warm and the cheese is melted.
If you'd like, you can slice the Bean and Cheese Burrito in half diagonally for easier handling.
Serve the burritos immediately.
Kids can enjoy their homemade Bean and Cheese Burritos with sour cream or salsa if desired.

English Muffin Pizzas

Ingredients:

2 English muffins, split in half (total of 4 halves)
1 2 cup pizza sauce or tomato sauce
1 cup shredded mozzarella cheese
1 4 cup sliced pepperoni or any preferred pizza toppings (e.g. sliced bell peppers, sliced olives, sliced mushrooms)
Dried oregano or Italian seasoning (optional, for seasoning)
Red pepper flakes (optional, for added spice)

Instructions:
Preheat the Oven:
Preheat your oven to 375°F (190°C).
Split the English muffins in half to create 4 halves.
Place the English muffin halves on a baking sheet or oven-safe tray.
Spread a spoonful of pizza sauce evenly over each English muffin half.
Sprinkle shredded mozzarella cheese on top of the sauce.
Add your choice of pizza toppings, such as pepperoni or any other preferred toppings.
If your child likes, sprinkle a pinch of dried oregano or Italian seasoning over the pizzas for added flavor.
For a bit of spice, you can also add a pinch of red pepper flakes.
Place the baking sheet in the preheated oven and bake for about 8-10 minutes or until the cheese is melted and bubbly, and the edges of the English muffins are golden brown
Carefully remove the English Muffin Pizzas from the oven using oven mitts. Let them cool for a minute or two.
Serve the mini pizzas while they're hot, and enjoy your homemade English Muffin Pizzas!

Chicken Parmesan Subs

Ingredients:
For the Chicken:
2 boneless, skinless chicken breasts
1 cup all-purpose flour
2 large eggs
1 cup breadcrumbs (Italian-style if available)
1/2 cup grated Parmesan cheese
Salt and pepper to taste
Cooking oil for frying
For the Assembly:
4 sub rolls or baguette pieces
1 cup marinara sauce (store-bought or homemade)
11/2 cups shredded mozzarella cheese
1/4 cup grated Parmesan cheese
Fresh basil leaves or parsley for garnish (optional)

Instructions:
Preparing the Chicken:
Preheat your oven to 375°F (190°C).
Set up a breading station with three shallow dishes. In the first dish, place the all-purpose flour. In the second dish, beat the eggs. In the third dish, combine the breadcrumbs, grated Parmesan cheese, salt, and pepper.
Dredge each chicken breast in the flour, ensuring it's coated evenly.
Dip the floured chicken into the beaten eggs, allowing any excess to drip off.
Coat the chicken with the breadcrumb mixture, pressing the breadcrumbs onto the chicken to adhere
In a large skillet, heat about 2 tablespoons of cooking oil over medium-high heat.
Add the breaded chicken breasts and cook for about 3-4 minutes on each side or until they are golden brown and crispy.
Transfer the fried chicken to a paper towel-lined plate to remove excess oil.
Assembling the Chicken Parmesan Subs:
Prepare the Sub Rolls:
Slice the sub rolls or baguette pieces open lengthwise, but leave them attached on one side, creating a pocket.
Spread marinara sauce inside each sub roll.
Place a chicken breast inside each sub roll.
Sprinkle shredded mozzarella cheese and grated Parmesan cheese over the chicken.
Place the assembled subs on a baking sheet.
Bake in the preheated oven for about 10-12 minutes or until the cheese is melted and bubbly.
If desired, garnish the subs with fresh basil leaves or parsley.
Serve the Chicken Parmesan Subs hot, and enjoy this delicious meal!

Pasta e Fagioli

Ingredients:
2 tablespoons olive oil
1 small onion, finely chopped
2 cloves garlic, minced
2 carrots, peeled and diced
2 celery stalks, diced
1 can (14 ounces) diced tomatoes
1 can (14 ounces) white beans (cannellini
or great northern beans), drained and
rinsed
4 cups chicken or vegetable broth
1 cup small pasta (such as ditalini or small
elbow macaroni)
1 teaspoon dried Italian seasoning (or a
mix of dried basil, oregano, and thyme)
Salt and black pepper to taste
Grated Parmesan cheese for serving
Fresh basil or parsley leaves for garnish
(optional)

Instructions:
In a large soup pot or Dutch oven, heat the olive oil over medium heat. Add the chopped onion, minced garlic, diced carrots, and diced celery. Cook for about 5-7 minutes, or until the vegetables start to soften.
Pour in the diced tomatoes (with their juice) and the drained and rinsed white beans. Stir well to combine.
Add the chicken or vegetable broth to the pot. Stir in the dried Italian seasoning (or herbs of your choice). Bring the soup to a boil, then reduce the heat to low. Let it simmer for about 10-15 minutes, allowing the flavors to meld together.
While the soup is simmering, in a separate pot, cook the small pasta according to the package instructions until al dente. Drain and set aside.
Add the cooked pasta to the soup and stir to combine. Let the soup simmer for an additional 5 minutes to heat the pasta through.
Taste the Pasta e Fagioli and season with salt and black pepper to your liking.
Ladle the hot soup into bowls. If desired, top each serving with grated Parmesan cheese and fresh basil or parsley leaves.
Serve the Pasta e Fagioli hot, and enjoy this hearty and comforting Italian soup!
This Pasta e Fagioli recipe is not only delicious but also versatile. Kids can have fun helping with chopping vegetables and stirring the ingredients together. It's a perfect warm meal for a cozy family lunch

Dinner

Cheese Ramen

Ingredients:
2 packs of ramen noodles
(without the seasoning packets)
2 cups water
1 cup milk (whole or 2% milk
works best)
1 1/2 cups shredded cheddar
cheese (or your favorite cheese)
2 tablespoons butter
Salt and pepper to taste
Optional toppings: sliced green
onions, cooked bacon bits, or
cooked and diced chicken

Instructions:
In a medium-sized saucepan, bring 2 cups of water to a boil.
Once the water is boiling, add the ramen noodles and cook them according to the package instructions, usually for about 3-4 minutes. Stir occasionally to prevent sticking.
Drain the cooked ramen noodles and set them aside.
In the same saucepan, melt the butter over medium heat.
Pour in the milk and heat it until it's hot but not boiling.
Gradually add the shredded cheddar cheese, stirring continuously until the cheese is fully melted and the sauce is smooth and creamy.
Add the cooked and drained ramen noodles to the cheese sauce in the saucepan.
Gently toss the noodles in the cheese sauce until they are evenly coated.
Season the Cheese Ramen with salt and pepper to taste. Be cautious with the salt, as cheese can be salty.
If you like, you can add sliced green onions, cooked bacon bits, or cooked and diced chicken on top for extra flavor and texture.
Serve the Cheese Ramen hot, and enjoy your creamy and cheesy comfort food!
This Cheese Ramen recipe is simple and can be customized with your favorite toppings. It's a great way to introduce kids to cooking, and they can have fun personalizing their cheesy ramen bowls. Please supervise them when using the stovetop for safety.

Easy Tomato Sandwich

Ingredients:

2 slices of bread (your choice, but whole wheat or multigrain works well)
1-2 ripe tomatoes, thinly sliced
2-3 lettuce leaves
Mayonnaise or mustard (optional)
Salt and pepper to taste

Instructions:

Prepare the Ingredients:
Wash and thinly slice the ripe tomatoes. Wash and pat dry the lettuce leaves.
If you prefer your sandwich with toasted bread, you can lightly toast the slices in a toaster or toaster oven. This step is optional.
Lay out the two slices of bread on a clean surface.
If you like, spread a thin layer of mayonnaise or mustard on one or both slices of bread. You can also leave the bread plain if you prefer.
Place the lettuce leaves on one slice of bread.
Arrange the thinly sliced tomatoes on top of the lettuce.
Sprinkle a pinch of salt and pepper over the tomatoes for added flavor.
Carefully bring the two slices of bread together to close the sandwich.
If desired, you can slice the Easy Tomato Sandwich diagonally or into smaller pieces for easier handling.
Serve the sandwich immediately, and enjoy your quick and refreshing Easy Tomato Sandwich!

Easy Cheese Quesadilla

Ingredients:

2 large flour tortillas (8-10 inches in diameter)
1 1/2 cups shredded cheddar cheese or your favorite cheese
Cooking spray or a small amount of melted butter (for cooking)

Instructions:
Prepare the Ingredients:
Have the shredded cheese ready.
Lay one tortilla flat on a clean surface.
Sprinkle an even layer of shredded cheese over the entire surface of the tortilla.
Heat a non-stick skillet or frying pan over medium-low heat.
If you like, you can lightly grease the skillet with cooking spray or a small amount of melted butter for added flavor.
Carefully place the assembled tortilla with cheese in the skillet.
Cook the quesadilla for about 2-3 minutes on one side or until the bottom tortilla is golden brown and the cheese starts to melt.
If you prefer, you can fold the tortilla in half to create a half-moon shape.
Using a spatula, carefully flip the quesadilla to cook the other side. Cook for another 2-3 minutes until it's golden brown and the cheese is fully melted
Carefully remove the quesadilla from the skillet and place it on a cutting board.
Use a sharp knife or pizza cutter to slice the quesadilla into wedges or triangles.
Plate the quesadilla slices.
Serve the Easy Cheese Quesadilla immediately, and enjoy your delicious cheesy treat!

Turkey Hummus Wrap

Ingredients:
1 large whole-grain or spinach
tortilla (10-12 inches in diameter)
2-3 tablespoons hummus (plain or
flavored)
2-3 slices of roasted turkey breast
1/4 cup shredded lettuce or
spinach leaves
1/4 cup thinly sliced cucumber
1/4 cup thinly sliced bell peppers
(red, green, or both)
1-2 slices of tomato (optional)
Salt and pepper to taste
Sliced avocado (optional)
Cheese slices (optional)
Mustard or mayonnaise (optional)

Instructions:
Wash and prepare the vegetables by slicing the cucumber and bell peppers. Set them aside.
Lay out the large tortilla on a clean surface
Spread a layer of hummus evenly over the entire surface of the tortilla, leaving a small border
around the edges.
Place the roasted turkey slices on top of the hummus.
Add the shredded lettuce or spinach, thinly sliced cucumber, and bell pepper strips on top of the
turkey.
If you like, add tomato slices, avocado slices, cheese slices, or any other preferred toppings for extra
flavor and texture
Sprinkle a pinch of salt and pepper over the vegetables for added flavor.
If desired, add a small amount of mustard or mayonnaise to the other side of the tortilla for extra
moisture and flavor.
Carefully roll up the tortilla tightly from the bottom, tucking in the sides as you go to create a compact
wrap.
Use a sharp knife to cut the Turkey Hummus Wrap in half diagonally or into smaller pieces for easier
handling.
Serve the wrap immediately, and enjoy your healthy and delicious Turkey Hummus Wrap!

Mac and Cheese

Ingredients:
8 ounces (about 2 cups) elbow macaroni or any pasta of your choice
2 cups shredded cheddar cheese (or a mix of cheddar and mozzarella for creaminess)
1/2 cup milk (whole or 2% milk works best)
2 tablespoons butter
1/2 teaspoon salt (or to taste)
1/4 teaspoon black pepper (optional, for added flavor)
1/4 teaspoon paprika (optional, for a subtle smoky flavor)

Instructions
In a large pot, bring water to a boil. Add a pinch of salt if desired.
Add the elbow macaroni or your chosen pasta and cook according to the package instructions until al dente. This usually takes about 8-10 minutes. Stir occasionally to prevent sticking.
Drain the cooked pasta and set it aside.
In the same pot, melt the butter over medium-low heat
Once the butter is melted, add the milk and stir to combine.
Gradually add the shredded cheddar cheese while continuing to stir. Keep stirring until the cheese is fully melted and the sauce is smooth.
If you like, season the cheese sauce with salt, black pepper, and paprika to taste. Stir until well combined.
Add the drained pasta back into the pot with the cheese sauce.
Gently stir the pasta and cheese sauce together until the pasta is well coated.
Cook the Mac and Cheese over low heat for a few minutes, stirring occasionally, until it's heated through.
Serve the Mac and Cheese hot, and enjoy your creamy and cheesy comfort food!

Grilled Cheese Roll Ups

Ingredients:
4 slices of bread (white,
whole wheat, or your
choice)
4 slices of American cheese
or your favorite cheese
2 tablespoons butter,
melted
Optional: Dipping sauce
(ketchup, marinara sauce,
or ranch dressing)

Instructions:
Lay out the slices of bread and cheese.
Use a rolling pin to gently flatten each slice of bread. This will make it easier to roll.
Place a slice of cheese on each flattened bread slice.
Carefully roll up each slice of bread with the cheese inside, starting from one end and
rolling toward the other end. Press lightly to seal the seam.
Brush the outside of each rolled-up sandwich with melted butter. This will help them
become crispy when cooked
Heat a non-stick skillet or frying pan over medium heat.
Place the roll-ups seam-side down in the skillet.
Cook for about 2-3 minutes on each side or until they are golden brown and the cheese
inside is melted. You can use a spatula to gently press them down to help them cook
evenly.
Carefully remove the Grilled Cheese Roll-Ups from the skillet and let them cool for a
minute or two. This will help the cheese inside set a bit.
Use a sharp knife to slice the roll-ups into bite-sized pieces or leave them whole.
If desired, serve the Grilled Cheese Roll-Ups with your favorite dipping sauce, such as
ketchup, marinara sauce, or ranch dressing.
Enjoy your Grilled Cheese Roll-Ups as a fun and tasty snack or meal!

Mild Chicken Fajitas for Kids

Ingredients:

For the Chicken Marinade:
1 pound boneless, skinless chicken breasts, cut into thin strips
2 tablespoons olive oil
1 teaspoon chili powder
1/2 teaspoon cumin
1/2 teaspoon paprika
1/2 teaspoon garlic powder
1/2 teaspoon onion powder
Salt and pepper to taste
Juice of 1 lime
For the Fajita Fixings:
1 bell pepper, thinly sliced (red or green)
1 onion, thinly sliced
1 cup sliced mushrooms (optional)
1 cup shredded cheddar cheese
1 cup sour cream or plain Greek yogurt
8 small flour tortillas
Salsa (mild or medium, depending on preference)

Instructions:

In a bowl, combine the olive oil, chili powder, cumin, paprika, garlic powder, onion powder, salt, pepper, and lime juice.

Add the chicken strips to the marinade and toss to coat evenly. Cover and refrigerate for at least 30 minutes to let the flavors meld.

Heat a large skillet over medium-high heat. Add a little olive oil if needed.

Add the marinated chicken strips to the skillet and cook for about 5-7 minutes, or until they are cooked through and no longer pink in the center.

Remove the chicken from the skillet and set it aside.

In the same skillet, add a bit more olive oil if needed, then add the sliced bell pepper, onion, and mushrooms (if using). Sauté them for about 5 minutes or until they are tender-crisp.

Warm the flour tortillas in the microwave or on a dry skillet for a few seconds.

Lay out each tortilla, and start by placing a portion of the cooked chicken strips in the center.

Add a generous scoop of sautéed vegetables on top of the chicken.

Sprinkle shredded cheddar cheese over the chicken and veggies.

Fold the sides of the tortilla over the filling, then fold up the bottom and roll it tightly to create a fajita.

Serve the Mild Chicken Fajitas with sour cream, salsa, and any additional toppings your child likes.

Veggie Pita Pizza

Ingredients:

4 whole wheat pita bread rounds
1/2 cup tomato sauce or pizza
sauce
1 cup shredded mozzarella cheese
Assorted veggies for toppings (e.g.,
bell peppers, cherry tomatoes,
sliced olives, sliced mushrooms,
thinly sliced red onion, sliced
spinach leaves)
Olive oil (optional, for drizzling)
Dried oregano or Italian seasoning
(optional, for seasoning)

Instructions:
Preheat your oven to 375°F (190°C).
Prepare the Pita Bread:
Lay out the pita bread rounds on a baking sheet or oven-safe tray.
Spread the Sauce:
Spread a layer of tomato sauce or pizza sauce evenly over each pita bread round, leaving a small
border around the edges.s:
Sprinkle shredded mozzarella cheese over the sauce on each pita.
Arrange your choice of veggies on top of the cheese. You can get creative and add a variety of colorful
veggies.
If you like, drizzle a small amount of olive oil over the veggies for added flavor.
Sprinkle a pinch of dried oregano or Italian seasoning on top of the pizzas for extra seasoning.
Place the baking sheet in the preheated oven and bake for about 10-12 minutes or until the cheese is
melted and bubbly, and the edges of the pita bread are golden brown
Carefully remove the Veggie Pita Pizzas from the oven using oven mitts. Let them cool for a minute or
two.
Use a sharp knife or pizza cutter to slice the pita pizzas into wedges or smaller pieces for easier
handling.
Serve the Veggie Pita Pizzas hot, and enjoy your homemade, healthy, and delicious pizzas!

Muffin Pan Frittatas

Ingredients:

Cooking spray or melted butter for greasing the muffin pan
6 large eggs
1/4 cup milk
Salt and pepper to taste
1/2 cup diced bell peppers (red, green, or both)
1/2 cup diced tomatoes
1/2 cup diced cooked ham or cooked bacon bits (optional)
1/2 cup shredded cheddar cheese
Fresh chives or parsley for garnish (optional)

Instructions:
Preheat your oven to 375°F (190°C). Grease a 12-cup muffin pan with cooking spray or melted butter.
Prepare the Ingredients:
Dice the bell peppers, tomatoes, and any optional ingredients like ham or bacon.
In a mixing bowl, whisk together the eggs, milk, salt, and pepper until well combined.
Divide the diced bell peppers, tomatoes, and any optional ingredients evenly among the greased muffin cups.
Sprinkle shredded cheddar cheese over the ingredients in each cup.
Carefully pour the egg mixture into each muffin cup, filling them about two-thirds full. The eggs will puff up while baking.
Place the muffin pan in the preheated oven and bake for approximately 15-20 minutes or until the frittatas are set and slightly golden on top.
Remove the muffin pan from the oven and let the frittatas cool for a few minutes.
If desired, garnish with fresh chives or parsley for a pop of color and flavor
Use a butter knife or small spatula to carefully lift the muffin pan frittatas out of the cups.
Serve the Muffin Pan Frittatas warm, and enjoy your delicious and portable breakfast!

Healthy Snacks

Berry Granola Frozen Yogurt

Ingredients:

2 cups plain Greek yogurt
2 cups mixed berries (such as strawberries, blueberries, raspberries)
1/4 cup honey or maple syrup (adjust to taste)
1/2 cup granola (your choice of flavor)
1 teaspoon vanilla extract (optional)

Instructions:

Prepare the Berries: Wash the mixed berries thoroughly and pat them dry. If using strawberries, remove the stems and chop them into smaller pieces.

Blend Berries and Sweetener: In a blender or food processor, combine the mixed berries and honey (or maple syrup). Blend until you have a smooth berry puree. Taste and adjust the sweetness if needed.

Mix Yogurt and Berry Puree: In a mixing bowl, combine the plain Greek yogurt with the berry puree. If desired, add vanilla extract for extra flavor. Mix well until the yogurt and berry puree are fully incorporated.

Layer the Mixture: In a freezer-safe container or loaf pan, layer the yogurt-berry mixture with granola. Start with a layer of the yogurt mixture, followed by a sprinkle of granola. Repeat the layers until the container is filled.

Swirl the Layers: Use a spoon or a knife to gently swirl the layers together, creating a marbled effect.

Freeze: Cover the container with plastic wrap or a lid and place it in the freezer. Allow the mixture to freeze for about 4-6 hours, or until it's firm.

Serve: Once the frozen yogurt is set, scoop it into bowls or cups. Top each serving with an extra sprinkle of granola for added crunch.

Enjoy: Your Berry Granola Frozen Yogurt is ready to enjoy! It's a delightful blend of creamy yogurt, sweet berries, and crunchy granola.

Storage: If you have any leftovers, keep them stored in an airtight container in the freezer. Allow the frozen yogurt to sit at room temperature for a few minutes to soften slightly before scooping and serving.

Feel free to customize this recipe by using your favorite type of berries and granola. You can also add other mix-ins like chopped nuts or mini chocolate chips for extra texture and flavor.

Homemade Fruit Roll-Ups

Ingredients:

2 cups ripe fruit (berries, peaches, mangoes, etc.)
1-2 tablespoons honey or maple syrup (optional, for added sweetness)
1 teaspoon lemon juice (for fruit flavor and preservation)

Instructions:

Prepare the Fruit: Wash, peel, and pit the fruit as needed. Cut it into smaller pieces for easier blending.

Blend the Fruit: Place the fruit pieces in a blender or food processor. Add honey or maple syrup if you want to enhance the sweetness. Blend until you have a smooth fruit puree.

Add Lemon Juice: Add lemon juice to the fruit puree and blend briefly. Lemon juice helps enhance the fruit's flavor and acts as a natural preservative.

Preheat Oven: Preheat your oven to the lowest possible temperature setting. This is usually around 140°F (60°C). If your oven doesn't go this low, you can use a food dehydrator if you have one.

Prepare Baking Sheet: Line a baking sheet with parchment paper. Make sure it fits comfortably inside your oven.

Spread the Fruit Puree: Pour the fruit puree onto the prepared baking sheet. Use a spatula to spread it into a thin, even layer. Try to keep the thickness as consistent as possible to ensure even drying.

Bake or Dehydrate: Place the baking sheet in the preheated oven. Leave the oven door slightly ajar to allow moisture to escape. The fruit puree will need to dry for several hours, depending on the thickness and water content of the puree. This can take anywhere from 4 to 8 hours.

Check for Doneness: The fruit puree is ready when it's no longer sticky to the touch but still pliable. It should be tacky but not wet.

Cool and Cut: Once the fruit puree is dried, remove it from the oven and let it cool for a few minutes. Gently peel it off the parchment paper and place it on a clean surface. Use kitchen scissors or a knife to cut it into strips or shapes.

Roll Up: Carefully roll up each strip or shape into a roll-up form. If desired, you can place a piece of parchment paper between each roll-up to prevent sticking.

Store: Store the homemade fruit roll-ups in an airtight container at room temperature for a week or two. For longer storage, keep them in the refrigerator or freezer.

Enjoy: Homemade fruit roll-ups are a nutritious and fun snack. They're perfect for school lunches, hikes, or anytime you want a tasty and wholesome treat.

Feel free to get creative by using different combinations of fruits or adding spices like cinnamon or nutmeg to enhance the flavor. Enjoy your homemade fruit roll-ups!

Cinnamon Sugar Pretzels

Ingredients:

1 (16-ounce) bag of pretzels (mini pretzels, sticks, or twists)
1/2 cup unsalted butter, melted
1/2 cup granulated sugar
2 teaspoons ground cinnamon

Instructions:

Preheat Oven: Preheat your oven to 350°F (175°C).
Prepare Cinnamon Sugar Mixture: In a small bowl, combine the granulated sugar and ground cinnamon. Mix well to evenly distribute the cinnamon throughout the sugar.
Melt Butter: In a separate bowl, melt the butter in the microwave or on the stovetop until it's completely liquid.
Coat Pretzels: Place the pretzels in a large mixing bowl. Pour the melted butter over the pretzels and gently toss to coat them evenly.
Add Cinnamon Sugar: Sprinkle the cinnamon sugar mixture over the butter-coated pretzels. Again, gently toss the pretzels to ensure they are coated with the cinnamon sugar mixture.
Bake: Spread the coated pretzels in a single layer on a baking sheet or two. Bake in the preheated oven for about 10-15 minutes, stirring once or twice during baking. Keep an eye on them to prevent burning.
Cool: Once the pretzels are baked and coated in cinnamon sugar, remove them from the oven and let them cool on the baking sheet. The coating will crisp up as they cool.
Serve: Once cooled, transfer the cinnamon sugar pretzels to a bowl or an airtight container for storage.
Enjoy: These Cinnamon Sugar Pretzels are ready to enjoy! They're a wonderful sweet and salty snack that's perfect for parties, movie nights, or simply as a treat anytime.
Feel free to adjust the amount of cinnamon sugar based on your taste preferences. You can also experiment with different types of pretzels or even add a pinch of nutmeg or cloves to the cinnamon sugar mixture for extra warmth and flavor.

No-Bake Chocolate Peanut Butter Oatmeal Bars

Ingredients:

1 cup peanut butter (creamy or crunchy, as preferred)
1/2 cup honey or maple syrup
1/2 cup unsweetened cocoa powder
2 cups old-fashioned rolled oats
1 teaspoon vanilla extract
Pinch of salt (if using unsalted peanut butter)
Optional add-ins: chopped nuts, chocolate chips, dried fruit

Instructions:

Prepare Pan: Line an 8x8-inch (20x20 cm) baking pan with parchment paper, leaving some overhang on the sides to easily lift out the bars later.

Melt Peanut Butter and Sweetener: In a medium saucepan over low heat, warm the peanut butter and honey (or maple syrup) until they are melted and well combined. Stir frequently to prevent burning.

Add Cocoa Powder: Remove the saucepan from the heat and whisk in the unsweetened cocoa powder until the mixture is smooth.

Stir in Oats: Add the rolled oats to the peanut butter mixture. If desired, add a pinch of salt and vanilla extract. Mix until the oats are thoroughly coated and the mixture is evenly combined.

Add Optional Add-Ins: If you like, mix in chopped nuts, chocolate chips, or dried fruit to add extra texture and flavor to the bars.

Press Mixture into Pan: Transfer the mixture to the prepared baking pan. Use a spatula or your hands to press it firmly into an even layer.

Chill: Place the pan in the refrigerator and allow the mixture to chill for at least 2-3 hours, or until the bars are firm and set.

Cut into Bars: Once the bars are chilled and set, use the parchment paper overhang to lift them out of the pan. Place them on a cutting board and use a sharp knife to cut them into bars of your desired size.

Enjoy: Your no-bake chocolate peanut butter oatmeal bars are ready to enjoy! Store any leftovers in an airtight container in the refrigerator for up to a week.

Air fryer roasted potatoes

Ingredients:

Potatoes (russet, Yukon gold, or red potatoes)
Olive oil
Salt
Pepper
Optional seasonings: garlic powder, paprika, rosemary, thyme, etc.

Instructions:

Prep Potatoes: Wash and scrub the potatoes to remove any dirt. You can peel them if you prefer, but leaving the skin on adds extra texture and nutrients. Cut the potatoes into evenly sized pieces, about 1/2 to 3/4 inch (1 to 2 cm) cubes.

Dry Potatoes: Place the potato cubes on a paper towel ad pat them dry to remove excess moisture. Dry potatoes will become crispier in the air fryer.

Season Potatoes: In a bowl, toss the potato cubes with a drizzle of olive oil to lightly coat them. Add salt, pepper, and any optional seasonings you like, such as garlic powder, paprika, or herbs.

Preheat Air Fryer: Preheat your air fryer to 375°F (190°C) for a few minutes.

Air Fry Potatoes: Place the seasoned potato cubes in the air fryer basket in a single layer, leaving some space between them for even cooking. You may need to cook them in batches if your air fryer is small.

Cook Potatoes: Cook the potatoes in the preheated air fryer for about 20-25 minutes, shaking the basket every 5-10 minutes to ensure even cooking. The potatoes should be golden brown and crispy on the outside and tender on the inside.

Serve: Once the potatoes are cooked to your desired level of crispiness, remove them from the air fryer and transfer them to a serving dish. Sprinkle with additional salt and pepper if needed.

Enjoy: Air fryer roasted potatoes are ready to be served as a delicious side dish. They're perfect alongside grilled meats, burgers, or as a simple snack.

Vegetable nuggets

Ingredients:
2 cups mixed vegetables (such as carrots, peas, corn, broccoli, and cauliflower), finely chopped or grated
1 cup mashed potatoes
1/2 cup bread crumbs (plus more for coating)
1/2 cup grated cheese (cheddar, mozzarella, or your choice)
1 teaspoon garlic powder
1 teaspoon onion powder
1/2 teaspoon dried oregano
Salt and pepper to taste
1-2 eggs, beaten (for binding)
Olive oil or cooking spray
Optional: dipping sauces (ketchup, yogurt-based dip, etc.)

Instructions:

Prep Vegetables: Steam or boil the mixed vegetables until they are tender. Drain well and allow them to cool.
Mix Ingredients: In a mixing bowl, combine the finely chopped or grated mixed vegetables, mashed potatoes, bread crumbs, grated cheese, garlic powder, onion powder, dried oregano, salt, and pepper. Mix well until everything is evenly combined.
Form Nuggets: Take small portions of the mixture and shape them into nugget shapes using your hands. You can use a cookie cutter to create uniform shapes if desired.
Coat Nuggets: Roll each nugget in additional bread crumbs to coat them evenly. This will give them a crispy exterior when cooked.
Binding: Dip each coated nugget in beaten egg to help the breadcrumbs adhere and hold the nugget together during cooking.
Preheat Oven: Preheat your oven to 375°F (190°C).
Baking: Place the coated and egged nuggets on a baking sheet lined with parchment paper. Lightly brush or spray the nuggets with olive oil or cooking spray to promote browning and crispiness.
Bake: Bake the vegetable nuggets in the preheated oven for about 20-25 minutes, or until they are golden brown and crispy.
Serve: Once cooked, remove the vegetable nuggets from the oven and let them cool slightly. Serve them with your favorite dipping sauces.

Zucchini slice muffins

Ingredients:

2 cups grated zucchini (about 2 medium zucchinis)
1 cup grated cheese (cheddar or your preferred type)
1 cup self-rising flour
1/2 cup diced ham or cooked bacon (optional)
1/4 cup chopped fresh herbs (such as parsley, chives, or basil)
4 large eggs
1/2 cup milk
1/4 cup olive oil
Salt and pepper to taste

Instructions:

Preheat Oven: Preheat your oven to 350°F (175°C). Grease or line a muffin tin with paper liners.
Prepare Zucchini: Grate the zucchini and squeeze out any excess moisture using a clean kitchen towel or paper towels. This will prevent the muffins from being too watery.
Mix Dry Ingredients: In a large mixing bowl, combine the grated zucchini, grated cheese, self-rising flour, diced ham or bacon (if using), and chopped fresh herbs. Mix well to evenly distribute the ingredients.
Whisk Wet Ingredients: In a separate bowl, whisk together the eggs, milk, and olive oil until well combined. Season with salt and pepper to taste.
Combine Wet and Dry: Pour the wet mixture into the bowl with the dry ingredients. Stir gently until everything is just combined. Be careful not to overmix.
Fill Muffin Cups: Spoon the batter into the prepared muffin tin, filling each cup about 3/4 full.
Bake: Place the muffin tin in the preheated oven and bake for about 20-25 minutes, or until the muffins are golden brown and a toothpick inserted into the center comes out clean.
Cool: Once baked, remove the muffin tin from the oven and let the zucchini slice muffins cool in the tin for a few minutes. Then, transfer them to a wire rack to cool completely.
Serve: Your zucchini slice muffins are ready to be served! They can be enjoyed warm or at room temperature.

Carrot French fries with minted salt

For Carrot Fries:
4-5 large carrots, peeled and cut into thin fry-like strips
2 tablespoons olive oil
Salt and pepper to taste
Optional seasonings: garlic powder, paprika, cayenne pepper, etc.

For Minted Salt:
1/4 cup fresh mint leaves, finely chopped
1/4 cup coarse sea salt or kosher salt

Instructions:
Minted Salt:
Prepare Minted Salt: In a small bowl, combine the finely chopped fresh mint leaves and the coarse sea salt. Mix well to evenly distribute the mint flavor throughout the salt. Set aside.
Carrot Fries:
Preheat Oven: Preheat your oven to 425°F (220°C).
Prepare Carrots: Peel the carrots and cut them into thin, fry-like strips. Try to make the strips as uniform as possible for even cooking.
Coat with Olive Oil: Place the carrot strips in a bowl and drizzle with olive oil. Toss to coat the carrots evenly with the oil.
Season Carrots: Sprinkle salt, pepper, and any optional seasonings you like over the carrot strips. Toss again to ensure the seasonings are distributed.
Arrange on Baking Sheet: Line a baking sheet with parchment paper. Arrange the seasoned carrot strips in a single layer on the baking sheet, making sure they don't overlap.
Bake: Place the baking sheet in the preheated oven and bake for about 20-25 minutes, or until the carrot fries are golden brown and crispy, turning them halfway through to ensure even cooking.
Minted Salt Finish: Once the carrot fries are done baking, immediately sprinkle them with a pinch of the prepared minted salt while they're still hot. The heat will help the minted salt stick to the fries.
Serve: Your carrot French fries with minted salt are ready to be served! Enjoy them as a tasty and nutritious snack.

Banana, strawberry and Nutella delight

Ingredients:

2 ripe bananas, sliced
1 cup fresh strawberries, sliced
Nutella or hazelnut spread
Whipped cream (optional)
Chopped nuts (such as hazelnuts or almonds) for garnish (optional)

Instructions:
Prepare Fruit: Wash and slice the ripe bananas and fresh strawberries.
Assemble: In serving dishes or dessert glasses, start by layering a few slices of bananas at the bottom.
Add Strawberries: Add a layer of sliced strawberries on top of the bananas.
Add Nutella: Spoon a layer of Nutella over the strawberries. The amount of Nutella is based on your preference: you can use a generous or moderate amount.
Repeat Layers: Repeat the layers as desired, creating additional layers of bananas, strawberries, and Nutella.
Whipped Cream: If desired, top the dessert with a dollo of whipped cream for added creaminess.
Garnish: Sprinkle chopped nuts (such as hazelnuts or almonds) on top for added crunch and flavor.
Serve: Your banana, strawberry, and Nutella delight is ready to be served! Enjoy it immediately.

Sesame-crunch fish fingers with yoghurt sauce

Ingredients:

1 pound white fish fillets (such as cod or haddock), cut into finger-sized strips
1/2 cup all-purpose flour
2 large eggs, beaten
1 cup sesame seeds
Salt and pepper to taste
Cooking oil for frying

Instructions:
Prepare Dredging Station: Set up a dredging station with three shallow bowls. Place the flour in the first bowl, beaten eggs in the second bowl, and sesame seeds in the third bowl.
Season Fish: Season the fish strips with salt and pepper.
Coat Fish: Dredge each fish strip in the flour, then dip it into the beaten eggs, and finally coat it thoroughly with sesame seeds. Press the sesame seeds onto the fish to ensure they adhere well.
Fry Fish: In a large skillet, heat cooking oil over medium-high heat. Carefully place the coated fish strips in the hot oil and cook for about 2-3 minutes on each side or until the sesame coating is golden brown and the fish is cooked through. Transfer the cooked fish fingers to a plate lined with paper towels to absorb excess oil.

Summer salad sandwich

Ingredients:

For the Salad Filling:

1 cup mixed salad greens (such as
lettuce, spinach, arugula)
1/2 cup cherry tomatoes, halved
1/4 cucumber, sliced
1/4 red onion, thinly sliced
1/4 bell pepper, sliced
1/4 cup feta cheese, crumbled
Fresh herbs (such as basil,
parsley, or dill), chopped
Optional: olives, avocado slices,
roasted red peppers

Instructions:

Prepare Salad: In a bowl, combine the mixed salad greens, cherry tomatoes,
cucumber, red onion, bell pepper, feta cheese, and chopped fresh herbs. Toss the
ingredients together gently to mix.
Assemble Sandwich: Lay out the slices of bread. Spread a layer of hummus or
your chosen spread on each slice.
Add Salad Filling: Divide the prepared salad filling evenly among two slices of
bread, placing it on top of the spread.
Stack and Press: Place the other slices of bread on top of the salad-filled slices to
create sandwiches. Gently press down to hold the sandwich together.
Serve: Your summer salad sandwiches are ready to be served! You can cut them
in half for easier handling.

White bean burger

Ingredients:

For the Burger Patties:
2 cans (15 ounces each) white beans (such as cannellini beans), drained and rinsed
1/2 cup breadcrumbs (whole wheat or gluten-free)
1/4 cup finely chopped onion
2 cloves garlic, minced
1 teaspoon ground cumin
1 teaspoon paprika
1/2 teaspoon salt
1/4 teaspoon black pepper
1 tablespoon olive oil
1 tablespoon lemon juice
Optional: chopped fresh herbs (parsley, cilantro), hot sauce

For Assembly:
Burger buns
Lettuce, tomato slices, onion rings, and other burger toppings
Condiments of choice (mayonnaise, ketchup, mustard, etc.)

Instructions:

Prepare the Burger Patties: In a food processor, combine the drained and rinsed white beans, breadcrumbs, chopped onion, minced garlic, ground cumin, paprika, salt, and black pepper. Pulse until the mixture comes together but still has some texture.

Add Flavor: Add the olive oil and lemon juice to the mixture. If desired, add chopped fresh herbs and a dash of hot sauce for added flavor. Pulse again to incorporate.

Form Patties: Divide the mixture into equal portions and shape them into burger patties. You can make them as thick or as thin as you prefer.

Cook Patties: Heat a skillet or non-stick pan over medium heat. Add a bit of oil to the pan. Cook the burger patties for about 3-4 minutes on each side, or until they are golden brown and heated through.

Assemble Burgers: Toast the burger buns if desired. Place a lettuce leaf on the bottom bun, followed by a white bean patty. Top with tomato slices, onion rings, and any other burger toppings you like.

Add Condiments: Spread your choice of condiments (mayonnaise, ketchup, mustard, etc.) on the top bun before placing it on top of the assembled burger.

Serve: Your white bean burgers are ready to be served! Enjoy them with a side of salad, fries, or your favorite side dish.

Desserts

Pear, coconut and raspberry spelt muffins

Ingredients:

2 cups spelt flour
1/2 cup shredded coconut (unsweetened)
1 teaspoon baking powder
1/2 teaspoon baking soda
1/4 teaspoon salt
1 teaspoon ground cinnamon
2 large ripe pears, peeled, cored, and diced
1/2 cup fresh or frozen raspberries
1/2 cup coconut oil, melted
1/2 cup maple syrup or honey
2 large eggs
1 teaspoon vanilla extract

Instructions:

Preheat Oven: Preheat your oven to 350°F (175°C). Line a muffin tin with paper liners or grease the muffin cups.

Mix Dry Ingredients: In a large bowl, whisk together the spelt flour, shredded coconut, baking powder, baking soda, salt, and ground cinnamon.

Prepare Fruit: Dice the peeled and cored pears into small pieces. If using frozen raspberries, you can keep them frozen until just before adding them to the batter.

Combine Wet Ingredients: In another bowl, whisk together the melted coconut oil, maple syrup or honey, eggs, and vanilla extract until well combined.

Add Wet to Dry: Pour the wet mixture into the dry mixture and gently fold until just combined. Do not overmix: a few lumps are okay.

Fold in Fruit: Gently fold in the diced pears and raspberries into the muffin batter.

Fill Muffin Cups: Spoon the muffin batter into the prepared muffin cups, filling each cup about 2/3 full.

Bake: Place the muffin tin in the preheated oven and bake for approximately 18-22 minutes, or until a toothpick inserted into the center of a muffin comes out clean.

Cool: Once baked, remove the muffins from the oven and let them cool in the tin for a few minutes before transferring them to a wire rack to cool completely.

Serve: Your pear, coconut, and raspberry spelt muffins are ready to be enjoyed! Serve them as a delightful breakfast or snack.

Banana berry yoghurt muffins

Ingredients:

1 1/2 cups all-purpose flour
1 teaspoon baking powder
1/2 teaspoon baking soda
1/4 teaspoon salt
1/2 teaspoon ground cinnamon
2 ripe bananas, mashed
1/2 cup plain Greek yogurt
1/2 cup granulated sugar
1/4 cup vegetable oil or melted coconut oil
1 large egg
1 teaspoon vanilla extract
1 cup mixed berries (such as blueberries, raspberries, or strawberries), fresh or frozen

Instructions:

Preheat Oven: Preheat your oven to 350°F (175°C). Line a muffin tin with paper liners or grease the muffin cups.

Mix Dry Ingredients: In a large bowl, whisk together the flour, baking powder, baking soda, salt, and ground cinnamon.

Prepare Wet Ingredients: In another bowl, combine the mashed bananas, Greek yogurt, granulated sugar, oil, egg, and vanilla extract. Mix well until the wet ingredients are thoroughly combined.

Combine Wet and Dry: Pour the wet mixture into the bowl with the dry ingredients. Gently fold and stir until just combined. Do not overmix: a few lumps are okay.

Add Berries: Gently fold in the mixed berries into the muffin batter.

Fill Muffin Cups: Spoon the muffin batter into the prepared muffin cups, filling each cup about 2/3 full.

Bake: Place the muffin tin in the preheated oven and bake for approximately 18-22 minutes, or until a toothpick inserted into the center of a muffin comes out clean.

Cool: Once baked, remove the muffins from the oven and let them cool in the tin for a few minutes before transferring them to a wire rack to cool completely.

Serve: Your banana berry yogurt muffins are ready to be enjoyed! They are moist, fruity, and perfect for breakfast or as a snack.

Fresh strawberry milkshake

Ingredients:

2 cups fresh strawberries, hulled and halved
2 cups cold milk (dairy or plant-based)
2-4 tablespoons granulated sugar, or to taste
1 teaspoon vanilla extract
Vanilla ice cream or frozen yogurt (optional)
Whipped cream and fresh strawberries for garnish (optional)

Instructions:

Prepare Strawberries: Wash the strawberries thoroughly, remove the stems, and cut them in half.

Blend Ingredients: In a blender, combine the fresh strawberries, cold milk, sugar, and vanilla extract. If you're using vanilla ice cream or frozen yogurt, you can add a scoop or two for extra creaminess and flavor.

Blend until Smooth: Blend the ingredients on high speed until the mixture is smooth and creamy. Taste and adjust the sweetness by adding more sugar if needed.

Check Consistency: Check the consistency of the milkshake. If it's too thick, you can add a bit more milk and blend again.

Serve: Pour the strawberry milkshake into glasses. If desired, top with a dollop of whipped cream and a fresh strawberry for garnish.

Enjoy: Your fresh strawberry milkshake is ready to be enjoyed! Serve it immediately while it's cold and refreshing.

Honey yoghurt tropical ice-blocks

Ingredients:

2 cups Greek yogurt (plain or vanilla-flavored)
1/4 cup honey, or to taste
1 cup mixed tropical fruits (mango, pineapple, kiwi, etc.), diced or sliced
Optional: shredded coconut, chopped nuts, or granola for added texture and flavor

Instructions:

Prepare Yogurt Mixture: In a bowl, combine the Greek yogurt and honey. Mix well until the honey is fully incorporated and the yogurt mixture is smooth and sweetened to your liking.
Prepare Tropical Fruits: Dice or slice the tropical fruits of your choice. You can use a combination of mango, pineapple, kiwi, or any other tropical fruits you prefer.
Assemble Ice-Blocks: If you have ice-block molds, layer the yogurt mixture and diced tropical fruits in the molds. Start with a layer of yogurt, followed by a layer of fruit, and continue until the molds are filled. Alternatively, you can mix the fruits directly into the yogurt mixture before pouring it into the molds.
Insert Sticks: If your ice-block molds require sticks, insert them into the molds according to the manufacturer's instructions.
Freeze: Place the molds in the freezer and allow them to freeze for at least 4-6 hours, or until the ice-blocks are completely frozen.
Serve: Once the ice-blocks are frozen, remove them from the molds by running the molds briefly under warm water to loosen them. Gently pull out the ice-blocks.
Optional Toppings: If desired, roll the edges of the ice-blocks in shredded coconut, chopped nuts, or granola to add texture and extra flavor.
Enjoy: Your honey yogurt tropical ice-blocks are ready to be enjoyed! They're a cool and delightful treat, perfect for hot days.

Berry smoothie ice-blocks

Ingredients:

2 cups mixed berries
(strawberries, blueberries,
raspberries, blackberries, etc.),
fresh or frozen
1 cup Greek yogurt or milk
(dairy or plant-based)
2-4 tablespoons honey or maple
syrup, or to taste
1 teaspoon vanilla extract
(optional)
Optional add-ins: banana slices,
chia seeds, spinach (for a
hidden veggie boost)

Instructions:

Blend Smoothie Mixture: In a blender, combine the mixed berries, Greek yogurt or milk, honey or maple syrup, and vanilla extract (if using). Blend until you have a smooth and creamy mixture.
Taste and Adjust: Taste the smoothie mixture and adjust the sweetness to your preference by adding more honey or maple syrup if needed.
Optional Add-Ins: If you'd like to add extra nutrients, consider adding a handful of baby spinach (for added greens), banana slices (for natural sweetness and creaminess), or a tablespoon of chia seeds (for added texture and omega-3 fatty acids). Blend again until smooth.
Fill Ice-Block Molds: Pour the smoothie mixture into ice-block molds, leaving a little space at the top for expansion as they freeze.
Insert Sticks: If your ice-block molds require sticks, insert them into the molds according to the manufacturer's instructions.
Freeze: Place the molds in the freezer and allow them to freeze for at least 4-6 hours, or until the ice-blocks are completely frozen.
Serve: Once the ice-blocks are frozen, remove them from the molds by running the molds briefly under warm water to loosen them. Gently pull out the ice-blocks.
Enjoy: Your berry smoothie ice-blocks are ready to be enjoyed! They're a cool and delicious treat, packed with the goodness of berries and dairy or dairy-free yogurt.

Fruit salad with honey yoghurt

Ingredients:

For the Fruit Salad:

Assorted fresh fruits (such as strawberries, blueberries, kiwi, pineapple, grapes, oranges, etc.), washed, peeled, and chopped as needed
Fresh mint leaves for garnish (optional)

For the Honey Yogurt:
1 cup Greek yogurt (plain or vanilla)
2-3 tablespoons honey, or to taste
1 teaspoon vanilla extract (if using plain yogurt)
Squeeze of fresh lemon juice (optional, to enhance flavors)

Instructions:

Prepare Fruits: Wash, peel, and chop the fresh fruits of your choice into bite-sized pieces. You can use a variety of colorful fruits to create a visually appealing salad.
Make Honey Yogurt: In a bowl, combine the Greek yogurt, honey, and vanilla extract (if using plain yogurt). Mix well until the honey is fully incorporated and the yogurt is sweetened to your liking. If desired, add a squeeze of fresh lemon juice to enhance the flavors.
Assemble Fruit Salad: Gently toss the chopped fruits in a large bowl to combine.
Serve: Serve the mixed fruits in individual serving dishes or a large serving bowl. Drizzle the honey yogurt over the fruits or serve it on the side.
Garnish: If desired, garnish the fruit salad with fresh mint leaves for a burst of freshness and color.
Enjoy: Your fruit salad with honey yogurt is ready to be enjoyed! Each spoonful combines the sweetness of the fruits with the creamy tanginess of the honey yogurt.

Banana energiser shake

Ingredients:

2 ripe bananas, peeled and sliced
1 cup milk (dairy or plant-based)
1/2 cup Greek yogurt
1 tablespoon almond butter or peanut
butter
1 tablespoon chia seeds or flaxseeds
1 tablespoon honey or maple syrup
(optional, for extra sweetness)
1/2 teaspoon vanilla extract
A pinch of ground cinnamon
(optional)
Ice cubes (optional)
Optional add-ins: protein powder,
spinach or kale (for a green boost),
oats (for extra fiber)

Instructions:

Blend Ingredients: In a blender, combine the sliced bananas, milk, Greek yogurt, almond butter or peanut butter, chia seeds or flaxseeds, honey or maple syrup (if using), vanilla extract, and ground cinnamon (if using). If you're adding any optional ingredients like protein powder or greens, add them as well.
Blend until Smooth: Blend the ingredients on high speed until the mixture is smooth and creamy. If you prefer a thicker shake, you can add a handful of ice cubes and blend again.
Taste and Adjust: Taste the shake and adjust the sweetness if needed by adding more honey or maple syrup.
Serve: Pour the banana energizer shake into glasses. You can garnish with a sprinkle of ground cinnamon or a drizzle of honey on top.
Enjoy: Your banana energizer shake is ready to be enjoyed! It's a nourishing and energy-boosting drink that's perfect for a quick breakfast or a post-workout refuel.

Raspberry & blueberry muffins

Ingredients:
2 cups all-purpose flour
1/2 cup granulated sugar
1/4 cup packed brown sugar
2 teaspoons baking powder
1/2 teaspoon baking soda
1/4 teaspoon salt
1/2 cup unsalted butter, melted
and cooled
2 large eggs
1 cup buttermilk (or substitute
with 1 cup milk + 1 tablespoon
vinegar)
1 teaspoon vanilla extract
1 cup raspberries, fresh or
frozen
1 cup blueberries, fresh or
frozen

Instructions:
Preheat Oven: Preheat your oven to 375°F (190°C). Line a muffin tin with paper liners or grease the muffin cups.
Mix Dry Ingredients: In a large bowl, whisk together the flour, granulated sugar, brown sugar, baking powder, baking soda, and salt.
Mix Wet Ingredients: In a separate bowl, whisk together the melted butter, eggs, buttermilk, and vanilla extract until well combined.
Combine Wet and Dry Mixtures: Pour the wet mixture into the bowl with the dry ingredients. Gently fold the ingredients together using a spatula until just combined. Do not overmix; a few lumps are fine.
Add Berries: Gently fold in the raspberries and blueberries. If using frozen berries, be careful not to overmix as they may release excess moisture.
Fill Muffin Cups: Divide the batter evenly among the muffin cups, filling each cup about 3/4 full.
Bake: Bake in the preheated oven for about 18-22 minutes, or until a toothpick inserted into the center of a muffin comes out clean or with just a few moist crumbs attached.
Cool: Remove the muffin tin from the oven and let the muffins cool in the tin for a few minutes. Then, transfer them to a wire rack to cool completely.
Enjoy: Once the muffins are completely cooled, they're ready to be enjoyed!

Healthy Peanut Butter Cookies

Ingredients:

1 cup natural peanut butter
(unsweetened, no added oils)
1/3 cup honey or maple syrup
1 large egg
1 teaspoon vanilla extract
1/2 teaspoon baking soda
A pinch of salt
Optional add-ins: dark
chocolate chips, chopped nuts,
chia seeds, flaxseeds, etc.

Instructions:

Preheat Oven: Preheat your oven to 350°F (175°C). Line a baking sheet with parchment paper.

Mix Ingredients: In a bowl, combine the natural peanut butter, honey or maple syrup, egg, vanilla extract, baking soda, and a pinch of salt. Mix well until all the ingredients are thoroughly combined.

Add Optional Add-Ins: If you're including any optional add-ins like chocolate chips or nuts, fold them into the cookie dough.

Form Cookies: Using a spoon or cookie scoop, portion out the cookie dough onto the prepared baking sheet. Use the back of a fork to gently press down on each cookie to create a criss-cross pattern.

Bake: Bake the cookies in the preheated oven for about 8-10 minutes, or until the edges are lightly golden.

Cool: Remove the baking sheet from the oven and let the cookies cool on the sheet for a few minutes before transferring them to a wire rack to cool completely.

Enjoy: Once the cookies are completely cooled, they're ready to be enjoyed!

Sides

Cheesy Cauliflower Breadsticks

Ingredients:

For the cauliflower crust:
1 medium head of cauliflower, florets separated
1 large egg
1 cup shredded mozzarella cheese
1/2 teaspoon dried oregano
1/2 teaspoon garlic powder
Salt and pepper, to taste
For the topping:
1/2 cup shredded mozzarella cheese
1/4 cup grated Parmesan cheese
1 teaspoon dried oregano

Instructions:

Preheat Oven: Preheat your oven to 400°F (200°C). Line a baking sheet with parchment paper.
Make Cauliflower Rice: Place the cauliflower florets in a food processor and pulse until they are finely chopped and resemble rice.
Steam Cauliflower Rice: Transfer the chopped cauliflower to a microwave-safe bowl and microwave on high for about 4-5 minutes, or until the cauliflower is tender. Let it cool slightly.
Drain Excess Moisture: Place the steamed cauliflower in a clean kitchen towel or cheesecloth and squeeze out as much moisture as possible. This step is important to prevent the crust from being too wet.
Mix Cauliflower Crust: In a bowl, combine the squeezed cauliflower, egg, shredded mozzarella cheese, dried oregano, garlic powder, salt, and pepper. Mix well to form a dough.
Shape the Crust: Transfer the cauliflower dough onto the prepared baking sheet and shape it into a rectangle or desired shape, about 1/4 inch thick.
Bake the Crust: Bake the cauliflower crust in the preheated oven for about 20 minutes, or until it's golden and firm.
Add Toppings: Remove the crust from the oven and sprinkle the shredded mozzarella cheese, grated Parmesan cheese, and dried oregano over the top.
Bake Again: Return the crust to the oven and bake for an additional 5-7 minutes, or until the cheese is melted and bubbly.
Slice and Serve: Let the cheesy cauliflower breadstick crust cool slightly before slicing it into breadstick-sized pieces. Serve with marinara sauce or your favorite dipping sauce.

Sweet potato chips

Ingredients:

2 medium sweet
potatoes
2 tablespoons olive oil
Salt and pepper, to taste
Optional seasonings
(paprika, garlic powder,
cayenne pepper,
rosemary, etc.)

Instructions:

Preheat Oven: Preheat your oven to 375°F (190°C).
Prepare Sweet Potatoes: Wash and peel the sweet potatoes. You can leave the skin on if you prefer, as it adds extra flavor and nutrients. Using a sharp knife or a mandoline slicer, slice the sweet potatoes into thin, even rounds. Thinner slices will result in crispier chips.
Toss with Oil: In a bowl, toss the sweet potato slices with olive oil, ensuring that each slice is coated evenly. You can do this by gently tossing with your hands or using a brush.
Season: Season the sweet potato slices with salt, pepper, and any optional seasonings of your choice. Popular options include paprika, garlic powder, cayenne pepper, or dried herbs like rosemary or thyme. Mix well to evenly distribute the seasonings.
Arrange on Baking Sheets: Arrange the seasoned sweet potato slices in a single layer on baking sheets lined with parchment paper. Avoid overcrowding to ensure even baking and crispiness.
Bake: Place the baking sheets in the preheated oven and bake for about 15-20 minutes. Check the chips after about 10 minutes and rotate the baking sheets if needed to ensure even cooking. The baking time can vary based on the thickness of the slices and your oven.
Monitor: Keep a close eye on the chips in the last few minutes of baking to prevent them from burning. The chips are done when they are golden brown and crispy.
Cool and Enjoy: Once the sweet potato chips are baked to your desired level of crispiness, remove them from the oven and let them cool on the baking sheets. They will continue to crisp up as they cool.
Store: Store the cooled sweet potato chips in an airtight container to maintain their crispiness.

Instant Pot Baby Potatoes

Ingredients:

1 pound baby potatoes,
washed and halved
1 cup water or
chicken/vegetable broth
2 tablespoons butter
2 cloves garlic, minced
1 teaspoon dried rosemary
(or your preferred herbs)
Salt and black pepper to taste
Chopped fresh parsley for
garnish

Instructions:

Prep the Potatoes:
Wash the baby potatoes and cut them in half. No need to peel them.
Sauté Garlic and Butter
Turn on the Instant Pot's "Sauté" function and melt the butter.
Add the minced garlic and sauté for about 1 minute until fragrant.
Add Potatoes and Seasonings:
Add the halved baby potatoes to the Instant Pot.
Sprinkle with dried rosemary, salt, and black pepper.
Add Liquid:
Pour in the water or broth. The liquid should cover the bottom of the Instant Pot.
Pressure Cook:
Close the Instant Pot lid and set the valve to the "Sealing" position.
Select the "Manual" or "Pressure Cook" function and set the timer for 4-5 minutes (depending on the size of your potatoes). Use the "High Pressure" setting.
Quick Release and Open Lid:
Once the cooking time is up, perform a quick pressure release by carefully turning the valve to "Venting."
When the pressure has released and the float valve drops, carefully open the lid.
Sauté (Optional):
If you prefer a bit of crispiness, you can use the "Sauté" function for a few minutes, stirring occasionally, until the potatoes are slightly golden and crispy.
Serve and Garnish:
Transfer the cooked potatoes to a serving dish.
Garnish with chopped fresh parsley.
Serve and Enjoy:
Instant Pot baby potatoes are ready to be served as a delicious side dish alongside your main course.
These Instant Pot baby potatoes are tender, flavorful, and infused with the aromatic butter and garlic. They make a perfect accompaniment to various meals, from grilled meats to roasted chicken.

63

Apple Nachos

Ingredients:
2-3 apples (any variety you prefer)
1/4 cup nut butter (peanut butter, almond butter, or your choice)
1/4 cup chocolate chips or chunks
1/4 cup chopped nuts (such as almonds, walnuts, or pecans)
1/4 cup dried fruit (raisins, cranberries, or chopped dates)
2 tablespoons honey or maple syrup
A sprinkle of cinnamon (optional)

Instructions:

Slice Apples: Wash and core the apples, then slice them thinly. You can leave the skin on for added texture and nutrition.

Arrange Apple Slices: Lay the apple slices in a single layer on a serving plate or a large platter, slightly overlapping them.

Drizzle Nut Butter: Warm the nut butter slightly to make it easier to drizzle. Drizzle the nut butter over the apple slices using a spoon or a small zip-top bag with a corner snipped off.

Add Toppings: Sprinkle the chocolate chips, chopped nuts, and dried fruit over the apple slices.

Drizzle Sweetener: Drizzle honey or maple syrup over the entire plate for added sweetness.

Optional Cinnamon: If you like, lightly sprinkle ground cinnamon over the nachos for extra flavor.

Serve Immediately: Apple nachos are best enjoyed right after assembling to prevent the apples from browning.

Enjoy: Grab a fork or simply use your hands to enjoy these delicious and creative apple nachos!

Vegetable kebabs

Ingredients:

For the Marinade:
2 tablespoons olive oil
2 tablespoons balsamic vinegar
1 teaspoon honey or maple syrup
1 teaspoon Dijon mustard
1 clove garlic, minced
1 teaspoon dried herbs (such as thyme, oregano, or rosemary)
Salt and black pepper to taste

For the Kebabs:

Assorted vegetables, such as bell peppers, red onion, zucchini, cherry tomatoes, and mushrooms, cut into bite-sized pieces
Wooden or metal skewers

Instructions:

Prepare the Marinade:
In a bowl, whisk together the olive oil, balsamic vinegar, honey or maple syrup, Dijon mustard, minced garlic, dried herbs, salt, and black pepper. This will be your marinade.
Prepare the Vegetables:
Cut the assorted vegetables into bite-sized pieces. Keep in mind that the vegetables should be similar in size to ensure even cooking.
Marinate the Vegetables:
Place the cut vegetables in a shallow dish or a resealable plastic bag.
Pour the marinade over the vegetables and toss gently to coat them well. Allow them to marinate for about 15-30 minutes.
Preheat the Grill:
Preheat an outdoor grill or stovetop grill pan over medium-high heat.
Assemble the Kebabs:
Thread the marinated vegetables onto the skewers, alternating the different types of vegetables for a colorful presentation.
Grill the Kebabs:
Place the vegetable kebabs on the preheated grill. Cook for about 10-15 minutes, turning the kebabs occasionally, until the vegetables are tender and have nice grill marks.
Serve:
Carefully remove the kebabs from the grill and transfer them to a serving platter.
Garnish and Enjoy:
Garnish the vegetable kebabs with some fresh herbs, if desired.
Serve the kebabs as a tasty and vibrant dish. They can be served on their own, with rice, or alongside your favorite dipping sauce.

65

Chargrilled courgettes with lemon & mint

Ingredients:
2 medium courgettes
(zucchini), sliced
lengthwise
2 tablespoons olive oil
Zest of 1 lemon
Juice of 1 lemon
2 tablespoons fresh mint
leaves, chopped
Salt and black pepper to
taste

Instructions:
Preheat an outdoor grill or stovetop grill pan over medium-high heat.
Slice the courgettes lengthwise into thin strips. You can also slice them diagonally for a different presentation.
In a bowl, combine the olive oil, lemon zest, lemon juice, chopped mint, salt, and black pepper.
Place the sliced courgettes in the bowl with the marinade. Toss them gently to coat them evenly with the mixture.
Place the marinated courgette slices on the preheated grill or grill pan. Grill for about 2-3 minutes on each side, or until they have distinct grill marks and are tender but not overly soft.
Transfer the chargrilled courgettes to a serving platter.
Sprinkle some additional chopped mint over the top for extra freshness and flavor.
Serve the chargrilled courgettes with lemon and mint as a delightful side dish. They pair well with grilled meats, fish, or as part of a Mediterranean-inspired meal.

Crispy Kale

Ingredients:

1 bunch of kale (about 6-8
large leaves)
1 tablespoon olive oil
Salt and seasoning of
your choice (such as
garlic powder,
nutritional yeast, chili
powder, etc.)

Instructions:
Preheat your oven to 350°F (175°C).
Prepare the Kale Leaves:
Wash the kale leaves thoroughly and pat them dry with a clean kitchen towel or paper towels.
Remove the tough stems from the kale leaves. Tear the leaves into bite-sized pieces.
Place the torn kale leaves in a large bowl.
Drizzle the olive oil over the kale leaves.
Gently massage the leaves with your hands to ensure they are evenly coated with oil. This helps to make
them crispy.
Sprinkle salt and your choice of seasoning over the kale leaves. You can use garlic powder, nutritional yeast,
chili powder, or any other preferred seasonings.
Arrange on Baking Sheet:
Line a baking sheet with parchment paper.
Arrange the seasoned kale leaves in a single layer on the baking sheet. Avoid overcrowding to ensure
crispiness.
Place the baking sheet in the preheated oven and bake for about 10-15 minutes, or until the kale leaves are
crisp and slightly golden. Keep an eye on them as they can burn quickly.
Once the kale chips are crispy, remove them from the oven and let them cool on the baking sheet for a few
minutes.
Serve and Snack:
Transfer the crispy kale chips to a serving bowl.
Enjoy them as a healthy and flavorful snack!

Crispy Broad Bean Skins

Ingredients:

Fresh broad bean pods
(fava beans)
Olive oil
Salt and seasonings of
your choice (such as chili
powder, paprika, garlic
powder, etc.)

Instructions:
Choose fresh broad bean pods that are plump and bright green in color.
Wash the pods thoroughly and pat them dry with a clean kitchen towel.
Open the pods by gently splitting them along the seam using your fingers or a small knife.
Remove the beans from the pods.
Carefully remove the outer skins (husks) from the beans. You can do this by gently pinching the skin
near the end where the bean was attached and sliding it off.
Lay the broad bean skins on a paper towel to remove excess moisture.Season the Skins:
In a bowl, drizzle the broad bean skins with a bit of olive oil and toss to coat them evenly. This will
help the skins become crispy during cooking.
Season the skins with salt and any other seasonings of your choice. You can use chili powder,
paprika, garlic powder, or other preferred spices.
Preheat your oven to about 350°F (175°C) or your air fryer to a similar temperature.
Spread the seasoned broad bean skins on a baking sheet or in the air fryer basket in a single layer.
If using the oven, bake the skins for about 15-20 minutes, flipping them halfway through, until they
are crispy and golden.
If using the air fryer, air-fry the skins for about 10-15 minutes, shaking the basket occasionally for
even cooking.
Once the broad bean skins are crispy, remove them from the oven or air fryer and let them cool
for a few minutes.
Serve the crispy broad bean skins as a crunchy snack. They are best enjoyed soon after cooking for
maximum crispiness.
Crispy broad bean skins can be a unique and tasty way to enjoy fava beans. They're a great
alternative to traditional potato chips and offer a satisfying crunch. Feel free to experiment with
different seasonings to create your desired flavor profile.

Thank you for choosing to embark on this culinary journey with me and for entrusting me with a small part of your kitchen adventures.

Your support and trust mean the world to me. Every recipe, every technique, and every story shared in this cookbook is a reflection of my passion for food and my desire to bring joy to your tables. Your decision to purchase this cookbook not only encourages me to continue sharing my culinary knowledge but also supports the countless hours of recipe testing, writing, and photography that went into its creation.

Wishing you many happy moments of deliciousness and culinary creativity!

For Zian And Milan, who brings smiles to my face and joy to my heart every day

Made in the USA
Las Vegas, NV
16 February 2024

85889264R00044